IN THE SALT MARSH

IN THE SALT MARSH

poems by

Nancy Willard

ALFRED A. KNOPF   NEW YORK   2004

THIS IS A BORZOI BOOK
PUBLISHED BY ALFRED A. KNOPF

www.randomhouse.com/knopf/poetry

Knopf, Borzoi Books, and the colophon are registered
trademarks of Random House, Inc.

The following poems have appeared in other publications:
"The Migration of Bicycles," "Niche Without Statue," and "The Boardwalk,"
Field; "Filming *The Time Machine* in the Twenty-first Century" and "Before
the Feast," *The Formalist;* "Houses," *The Hornbook;* "The Butterfly Forest,"
"Sky. Clouds. Apples.," "Choosing a Stone," "The Wonderful Lamp," and "An
Accident," *The Hudson Review;* "Little Journey" and "Rooms," *Image;* "The
Wish of the Brother with a Swan's Wing," *Lapis;* "Breakup on the Hudson,"
The Massachusetts Review; "In the Salt Marsh," "At Tivoli Bays," and "The
Snow Arrives After Long Silence," *The New Yorker;* "The Ladybugs,"
OneEarth; "The Drowned Man," *River City;* "Love in America,"
Witness; "The Training of the Retriever," *Yankee Magazine.*
The poems in "The River That Runs Two Ways" appeared in a
limited-edition book of that title published by the Brighton Press
in San Diego. They accompanied panoramic photographs
taken in the Hudson Valley by Eric Lindbloom.
Grateful acknowledgment is made to the National Council of Teachers of
English for permission to reprint "The Way She Left Us," previously published
under the title "The Journey," in *College English*, vol. 61, no. 1. Copyright ©
1998 by the National Council of Teachers of English. Reprinted by permission
of the National Council of Teachers of English.

Library of Congress Cataloging-in-Publication Data
Willard, Nancy.
In the salt marsh : poems / by Nancy Willard. — 1st ed.
p.   cm.
ISBN 1-4000-4229-1
1. Salt marshes—Poetry.   2. Nature—Poetry.   I. Title.
PS3573.I444I55 2004
811'.54—dc22
2003065887

Manufactured in the United States of America
First Edition

For Eric, who called me to the salt marsh

Contents

Private Lives of Public Places

The River That Runs Two Ways

Love in America

Love in America

When I paid for my flowers, six white roses,
the florist, Mrs. Abdoo, said, "Is this
your saint's day?"
She admired the gown I'd made in secret.
It brushed my knees, a white cotton dress
I'd wear for everyday after this wedding
with no priest to bless us, without my father
to give me away.

I'd give myself away to my first love,
photographer and grandson of the best
harness maker in Uppsala who sailed
to the New World and Detroit, where few loved
the sleek flesh and loyalty of horses
clop-clopping toward death. Flesh
is a poor investment. "What blessed weather
for your day," said Mrs. Abdoo, putting
a small box in my hands. "A wedding gift.
Open it together."

The white house of the justice of the peace
in Mabbettsville, New York, smelled of fresh paint.

His wife opened the door.
A black-and-white TV played Nixon's face.
Behind her, I caught sight of an old man
in bedroom slippers, sweeping the kitchen floor.
She asked if we'd brought extra witnesses.
"We need one more."

She called to the mailman. He agreed to serve.
My love and I sat on the sofa, waiting.
The justice changed into his marrying clothes:
a tie printed with small basset hounds,
a navy vest, and chocolate wing-tipped shoes.
Two continents away, we strafed a shore
I'd never heard of. Cut to the president:
"We seek no wider war."

The justice said, "Turn that thing off." His wife
switched off the sound. "Do you take this man"—
My love and I gave promises and rings.
Nixon kept making faces: *Love won't save you!*
Outside, we opened our first gift: this picture.
Our Lady of Good Voyages holds her son.

Her other hand offers a model ship—
the *Santa Maria* looked that small to God.
We stopped for gas. Outside I found a phone.
"Mama, I'm married. Papa, I love you both.

We're on our own."

The Ladybugs

It's true. I invited them into my home,
four thousand ladybugs from the Sierras.
I paid for their passage.
I paid for their skilled labor.
I was desperate when I read the notice
in a mail-order catalog showing flea zappers
and organic devices for vaporizing mold.

Are pests killing your trees and shrubs?
Ladybugs are the answer.

They arrived, famished and sleepy,
in a muslin bag slim as a pencil case,
or a reticule for opera glasses,
or very small change.
For once in my life I read the instructions
for sending my private army into the world.

The ladybugs will want a drink
after their long journey.
Sprinkle the sack before releasing them.

I shook handfuls of water over them.
Drops big as bombs pounded their shelter,

a mass baptism into our human ways.
They did not buzz or beat their wings,
but as the warmth of my house woke them,
I saw a shifting of bodies, of muscles rippling,
like waves adjusting themselves to a passing boat.

*Do not release the ladybugs during the heat of the day
or while the sun is shining.*

Under the full moon I carried my guests
to the afflicted catalpa waving its green flags.
I untied the bag. I reached in and felt a tickling,
a pulsing of lives small as a watch spring.
I seized a handful and tossed them into the branches.
They clung to my hand for safety.
Their brothers and sisters,
smelling the night air,
hung on my thumb, my wrist,
and my arm sleeved in ladybugs, baffled, muttering
in the silent tick of their language,
Where are we? What does she want of us?

*Do not release too many at one time.
A tablespoon of ladybugs on each shrub*

and a handful on each tree should keep them
pest-free. Keep on hand, always, a small bag
of ladybugs in your refrigerator.
Do not freeze.

I have made my abode with the ladybugs
and they have chosen me as their guardian,
because the meek shall inherit the earth,
because I found one at rest in the porch
of my ear, because I did not harm the one
that spent the night under the deep ridge
of my collarbone, or the one that crossed
my knuckles like a ring seeking
the perfect finger.

The Butterfly Forest

Sir, your scalp turns shy, yanked
into light, veiled by hair
so thinned by months of chemo
it lies like grass beaten flat
by the wind or the feet of trekkers
climbing away from the gardens,
the woods, the glad streams
toward the summit
where lives seen only in part
lie clear as cities asleep

under the gaze of pilots
ordered to bomb them. Today
you bustle us to this place
you have always wanted to see:
the butterfly forest
in the conservatory,
where the captives do not know
they are captive, so lush
is their prison: hibiscus

and roses and passion vine,
the air warm and moist
to keep the blood moving

in these cold-blooded vamps
taking their ease in a spa,
their silken kimonos
fluttering. The zebra longwings
surround us
like a sprinkle of flying masks.

The viceroy, brown
with mildewy spots, closes
his dull book but opens
for the patient reader;
the painted ladies
flicker their shadows like tongues
tasting good gossip
and a ghostly kiss on the cheek.
They ride on our shoulders,

our hair. When we leave,
even you shake off ghosts
whose lives are half over.
The eccentrics, the shy,
the perfectly groomed

in their tails and cloaks,
even the bright ones
we would love to wear
in our cold world
want us to carry them.

The Way She Left Us

Oh, ancient lady, I hope you are streaking to heaven
in new sneakers, your best broom in your hand.
If you were a tree, you would shade God's house,
but your ashes are meeker than unrisen bread
under the cloth stitched with a topaz cross.

When the priest pulls it away, you do not change
into a door or a dove or a plateful of light.
Sensible to the end, you keep to the cardboard box
he bears in both hands like a child trusted to carry
a glass of chilled champagne to an honored guest.

Your daughters and sons are flowing behind you,
and their sons and daughters, and children,
sisters and brothers, their mouths sealed with awe.
At the end of the garden, a shovel stands up
for itself in the bed knotted with pansies.

Where the loam raises its small fist,
the priest opens the box, his wrist turns,
and you sift out of sight into the world's weather,
but a curl of ash plumes out like a wish:
Let me go, children, and bless each other.

Phone Poem

If the phone rings in a dream, should I answer?
If I answer, who will hear me?
Can silence hear?
Do the dead make calls?

Is my father returning the call I made
so many years ago in a dream?
Does the operator who told me
the line was broken now call with good news,

that dead silence was only sleeping,
that beyond all names and all numbers,
beyond all known paths, beyond the pause
between heartbeats, between breath stopped

and the gap of his going,
she has found him waiting for news
of weather in the world he loved,
of new children learning to walk

on the sweet crust of the earth?
Will he hear my message?
If I hear silence,
is the silence listening?

Houses

My father's house was made of sky.
His bookcases stood twelve feet high.
The snowy owl my father tamed,
the stones he showed me, stars he named,
agate, quartz, the Milky Way—
"It's good to know their names," he'd say,
"so when I'm gone and you are grown,
in any world you'll feel at home."

My mother's house was made of talk,
words that could rouse a flea to fight
or make a stone stand up and walk.
Words filled the kitchen day and night.
Grandpa knew all the Psalms by heart.
My mother's sisters knew the art
of telling tales, and lies so new
all those who heard them called them true.

My house is quieter than theirs.
My promises are frail as foam.
I still forget to say my prayers.
Between the lines I plucked this poem.
Look up. To the discerning eye,
my house stands open to the sky.

Filming *The Time Machine* in the Twenty-first Century

How flawlessly the Time Machine
winds itself up all afternoon
under its own electric moon,

with quiet flocks of learned men
in morning coats (nineteen years young)
and bowler hats and shoes well shined,
piano-black, like well-designed
reservoir pens that mark the snow,
record the past, and let it go.

And two young women cast in brown,
from woolen coats to buttoned gowns
hemmed in fresh snow, wait for their cues,
adjust their wraps,
and stroke the feathers in their caps.

Two walk-on parts, no lines to learn;
nineteen years young, they wait their turn,
like bells that want a woman's hand
to ring for servants. Dinner's late,
and Time is standing at the gate.

The Time Machine stands very small.

Without the sun, the moon, the sky,
you'd hardly notice it at all.

The movie camera cocks its eye.
The lights awake, and swooping low,
the long-stemmed microphonic flower
gathers the hiss of falling snow.
Those unrung girls, those boys in black—
what time dissolves, let film take back.
Oh, take the lie but make it true!
Take one—
Take two—

Choosing a Stone

The tide pulls back, leaving its cargo of stones
on the broad counter of sand.
A boy takes only black stones halved with a white thread,
like a parcel too private to open.
His mother gathers stones that mimic food:
two quartz eggs and a granite potato
and a loaf of bread with a cold crust.

This man hunts the white stones,
smooth as unblemished fruit
made, he feels, for his hand alone.
He picks one up, fingers a hairline crack.
Throws it back. This woman saves stones
on the verge of extinction. Thin as a cat's ear,
they shine like coins rubbed faceless
for luck, for safe crossing.

The Sandbar

In the country of scallops,
shy fans sleep under a quilt of water.
Alive, they applauded each other,
ashen or creamy, huffing their ribbed valves
over the cool floor.
Now the sandbar gathers their shells
from which so many sunrises hatched.

In the country of pandora clams,
improbable as the thumbnails of angels,
these paired petals fell from a garden of pearls
like syllables that click and shine
in the ancient language of light.

And here is the country of humans,
digging a hole and watching the tide take it,
or fighting a sea bass senseless, or saving
and sorting the sea's beautiful discards
(the moon snail's faded turban, the oysters
pressed to the mud flats like ears
eavesdropping on earthquakes),

or staking the pitcher's mound and home plate
on a sandbar till the outfielder runs knee-deep
in waves, the sea scrubs down the sand,
the sun strikes out, and humans
choose land.

A Human Error

All alone on the sand it stood.

A moon snail, big as a peach,
shining as if the sea lit it
to give the drowned a decent burial.
I admired its chalky armor, a house
for an anchorite polished with prayers,
or a slim girl tucked into a tower.

When the first wave covered it,
I thought of the tide, of moon snails broken
and tossed aside. I thought
of their corridors without footfalls,
of their turrets without pennants
cracked open to shadows and voices.
I thought of the morning light opening
and closing, and the stars rising.

I watched the sea place its beautiful coffin
on the dark page of the sand.
When the waves pulled back,
I sprang forward. I grabbed the moon snail.
The dark mushroom of its body
spilled into my hand like a velvet sleeve.

Its frilly flesh grasped mine. I threw it down.
Safe now, it tried to refold itself.

Uncrinkling its pleats, disordered by fear,
it sank, disheveled and blind, into sand,
as if through a trapdoor on a bare stage.
Does the taint of my hand haunt it?
Does its muscle remember me? Baffled
by light, by sweat, by a shape not its own,
does it go on smoothing itself like laundry,
washing me out of its simple body?

Apple

I am the magician's friend,
Northern Spy, Golden Delicious,
my skin a flawless fit,
flecked like a galaxy, streaked
like the sea in a spyglass
when waves close ranks
over the sun as it steps
into its cold bed.

Polished, I make my own light.
The bloom off, I am still beautiful.
I somersault. I roll over.
I sit on my haunches for hours.
I am the Mistress of Secrets.
Poison me. My flesh keeps quiet
and shows only its good side.
See! No hands.

No pockets. No secret passages.
No doors. Slice me, I hide
wheels but no gears.
Peel me, I uncoil without springs.
My stem does not wind
your hours.

Dip me in gold, I am a prize
for the winner.

Cut me in two.
Share me with your beloved.
With my body I marry you
under the full moon.

The Snow Arrives After Long Silence

The snow arrives after long silence
from its high home where nothing leaves
tracks or stains or keeps time.
The sky it fell from, pale as oatmeal,
bears up like sheep before shearing.

The cat at my window watches
amazed. So many feathers and no bird!
All day the snow sets its table
with clean linen, putting its house
in order. The hungry deer walk

on the risen loaves of snow.
You can follow the broken hearts
their hooves punch in its crust.
Night after night the big plows rumble
and bale it like dirty laundry

and haul it to the Hudson.
Now I scan the sky for snow,
and the cool cheek it offers me,
and its body, thinned into petals,
and the still caves where it sleeps.

The Wonderful Lamp

As it was very dirty, she began to rub it, that it might fetch a higher price. Instantly a hideous genie appeared and asked what she would have.

—ALADDIN AND THE WONDERFUL LAMP

Admire this lamp, hammered
from copper. It's odd

as an orthopedic shoe
or a coffin for bananas.

A protective tarnish darkens
the shining face it brought

into this world, after the smith
told his hands:

Let the Hidden One sleep,
and light his way
to the cave of stories.

The Wish of the Brother with a Swan's Wing

As soon as the shirts touched them, the swan skins fell off, and her brothers stood before her in the flesh. Only the youngest was missing his left arm, and he had a swan's wing on his shoulder instead.

—"THE SIX SWANS," *THE BROTHERS GRIMM*

To meet his left arm again.
To pick up pebbles and skip them.
To close ten fingers over a pearl
of great price. To wind the gold stem
of his watch. Or not wind it.
To stop time. To walk up and speak to her.
To play Chopin and move the minutes
to tears. To carve her name on a bench.
To lift her chin toward his mouth.
To dance with her, one hand at the small
of her back, the other clasping her fingers
lightly—they are so small, like the bones
of a bird! With his strong left hand,
to slip a gold band on her finger.
To throw off his shirt, blue as the asters,
that his sister wove from the wild stars
of the field. To be broken yet whole, a ring

of still water. To sleep with his bride
on the floor of a white boat as it floats
out to sea. To carry her on the water's
shoulders. To shelter her
under his wing.

Sky. Clouds. Apples.

I shall become a disciple of clouds,
windblown like the brushed wings of waves,
or heaped, dome upon dome, in eccentric hives,
or pulled like scenery crossing an empty sky.
I have seen fish in the sky and a dog
that sank into a sheep pursuing a bird
at so majestic a pace they hung like a frieze

of carved smoke, shading the mountain's flank,
and once, as a child, a white ship so grand
I called my mother to see it,
and she opened the kitchen door and stood
on the threshold and scanned the evening light
as it opened a hole in the canopy of maples
on the empty berth at the darkening wharf of the sky.

On my first trip to the sky, when the plane
· broke through the clouds I saw the ballrooms
of heaven with nobody in them, the floors swept clean
with brooms of light. No nomads so restless
as clouds. No saint so quick to surrender the self
over and over: *Love, and do you what you will.*
Wear me. I am already you.

Now storms are pruning the orchards.
The broken flesh of apples, scarred
or cut to the core, litter the green aisles.
This morning I saw clouds rise from the mowed field
where they camped all night under the mountain
and departed in sunlit coaches,
turning away, into the clean sky.

An Accident

Thunk. A goldfinch dropped to the deck,
her head bobbing, unstrung,
her buttery breast warm when I picked her up,
her left eye pushed back where it struck the glass,
the other open, black as a currant
but clouding over, like the day itself,

as I carried her in a clamshell serving again
as a coffin for a creature leaving its element.
I tucked up her feet and the wing splayed
by the blow. All afternoon my bird lay
in state on the glass table under the umbrella.

Her crushed eye sank deeper. A dropperful
of blood darkened and slicked her breast.
With night coming on, I fetched my bird
and closed her up in the shed
where the crows would not find her.

On the third day, maggots writhed in her belly
like a terrible birth, and I rushed her outside,
a black rag of herself. One wing stuck out

like a knife plunged through a scorched bun.
The fifth day brought rain. The maggots left
to start their own journey.

Your tail feathers loosened, one by one,
and your bones appeared in tatters of flesh.
May you wake in your next life as a glad bride
who turns to her groom and tells him her dream:
When I was a bird, the wind carried me,
and when I died, somebody said goodbye.

Deer Skull

—For Howard Knotts

Look at this skull you found in the woods.
Notice the lightning that maps a road from the jaw
packed with teeth to the gap under the bony roof
that guarded the deer's instincts, its hunger,
its memory of paths as hidden from sight
as the sinews binding the night sky
into Swan, Bear, Dipper, Southern Cross.

Look through the eye sockets, not at the loss
of sight but through windows, wide as a windshield.
Look through these moon-gates into the garden
of clouds, into the cave of planets
like holy beads breaking free
from their joyful mysteries
and crossing the heavens on their own journey.

Notice the flicker of fish, the petals dropped
like pages, the moon reading herself by her own light.
Now we are floating in the night sky,
crossing the Sea of Tranquillity in the ark of a skull.
Death steers, takes all tricks, saves nothing.
If the deer had not lived, it would not have died.
If you had not lived, you could not make this journey.

In the Salt Marsh

How faithfully grass holds the shape of the sea it loves,
how it molds itself to the waves, how the dried salt
peaks into cowlicks the combed mane of the marsh.
Tousled by tides, it pitches tents, breaks into turrets
and coxcombs and whorled nests and green baskets
for the bleached armor of fiddler crabs, like earrings
hung by the sea on lobes of darkness. Could I lay my ear
on that darkness where the tide's trowel smooths islands
and scallops the sand, moon-tugged, till it slows
and turns? Could I keep the past in the present's eye?
Could I know what the grass knows?

Private Lives of Public Places

The Migration of Bicycles

I have seen them flash among cars or lean
so low into the curved wrist of the road
to brake would kill them, yet a whole pack
will stand for hours in the rain

yoked to each other, chained to the rack
till the shops close. I have seen
them balanced on one foot like a clam,
the front wheel turned, at ease. It waits

like a severed centaur, for lover or thief
to give it a running push, shift gears, and ride
off with the Great Bear and the full moon
hooping the earth, winding the spring tide.

The Training of the Retriever

Her hand curves the ball, the tall grass catches it.
The dog sees where the arc of its flight took root
and wades in. The next time she aims for the water,
and the dog wrestles it from the suck of the sand

and brings it back and buries it in her hand,
its side caved in where his teeth bent it.
Count no more times. Pitted, bald as the moon,
it circles the planets, where her hand sent it.

Niche Without Statue

Somebody lived here. Stepped away. No tracks.
Open house to the air, an alcove scoured
to stucco light. No slippery foot. A shell.
This space was made for one whose shadow towered

over the common life. Light rings the bell,
steps in, leaves no tracks when she leaves,
and all night long, doesn't the sun recite
what the moon measures and the tide believes?

The Absence at the Swing

A long shadow, finding the park still,
lights on the jungle gym, the swing, the grass.
The absent have tamped it down. Their heels cut
diamonds, and broken halos shingle the sandy path.

The rabbit who feeds in stop-motion stays hidden
but watches the swing row back and forth and back.
Somebody sat here, warmed herself in the light,
and moved on, feeling the long shadow at her back.

Before the Feast

The hen is dressed to kill. For once in her life,
she travels in style. Her wings, sleepy as sherry,
fit in their pockets of flesh like folding knives.
She weighs so little. Caught in the cook's right hand,

she cocks her head, she shakes the light from her neck.
On the road home from market, the sun bakes
the cook in her own juice and salts her with sweat.
The stars blow themselves out. Now the oven wakes.

The Drowned Man

As the sea tightens its soft ropes and tows him,
he loses the white beach, seeded with bathers,
where, like a leaning sundial, his umbrella
adjusts the shade for him. Far off, waves lather

the sand, swabbing it clean, and lay him out
to dry on the wet shore like a battered kite
and show him a lamp cut from the bones of flowers
but not who carries it and snuffs the light.

The River That Runs Two Ways

The Boardwalk

Who called for this trail? Not the thrush, who needs none
and whose tongue has no peep or syllable for drown.
Not the water striders, who dance on the shroud of the
    drowned,
which is also the sky over the trout's nest.
The boardwalk is planked like a dock, it is what I need
to enter the freshwater marsh on the hem of the bay
and speak with the herons, who think I am one of them,
standing as still as they and fishing for what I love,
the poplar shaking the light off itself like a dog,
the muffled torches of cattails, the smokebush shaky as
    sand
and the water lilies in bud unpacking their crowns,
their round leaves slit, like clocks with one hour lost
and water sounds the same as the word for land.

At Tivoli Bays

At Tivoli Bays, where the rapes happened that spring,
tide pools shine in the crisp tracks of the deer
where I saw an island, thin as a tongue, its cargo
of bare saplings mudbound, paraded like captives,
moored in the shallows, standing room only, with barely
space for two women to walk. See the moon's thumb
whorled on the noon sky? Now the tide's turning
the Hudson out of its bed. Can you see the road?
Then you haven't walked far enough. If you come at dusk
you'll find the deer leaving their ample rooms,
their ears twitching, legs cocked to explode.

Little Journey

Darkness comes early now, and the maples light
the lamps they hid under their green shawls.
Has everyone left? It's grown so still in the orchard
among wooden boxes like coffins brimming with
    weather
and brooms of light clearing corridors under the trees
where the wheels of asters tick on the wrist of the wind
and the milkweed packs its silk in a green horn
and the curled fists of the Queen Anne's lace hoard seeds
and water shines in the scarred ruts where the wagons
    pass
the trees, old travelers, juggling their bright baggage,
those shoppers bearing gifts for the whole family,
though one tree stumbled, its roots kicking the light,
its apples at rest where they dropped, like balls freed
    from the game
when the sun slips away for one more look at the grass.

Breakup on the Hudson

The ice in Rhinebeck calls to the ice in Kingston
and below, a window cracks in the dim rooms
heavy with sleep, the sleepers in deep suspense
like the paraffin roof on a jar of summer preserves,

as if a dinghy that sank off Cold Spring
rolled restlessly in the open palm of the water.
What time turned off for the winter, what stopped
the dance of the shad, the lick and shine of the waves

opens now to faint applause. I eavesdrop
on distant thunder. I hear the ice cracking
a dirty joke as the sharp words break loose,
good loose talk letting the world back in.

In the Vineyard

Even the young look old, tendons stretched on the rack,
tendrils springing and coiling, arm grafted to arm,
survivors, a close-knit family bent to a single purpose,
hundreds of primitive hands passing buckets of water

to barns set ablaze by the sky. Oh, what would they do
with hands that grip and conceal?
What on earth would they save?
Not the grapes sealed with light like jade chandeliers,

not the darkness caught by petals chapeled in prayer,
not the dry applause from row after row watching
the ripe moon rise from its nest at the top of the hill,
motherless, fatherless, crossing the darkening field.

The Guardian

—For Frederick Franck

The one who lives in the garden is waiting for you.
She hides herself under the face she shows

to oaks and catalpas and birches. Covens of crows
gossip and preen. She shades the wren and the jay,

letting them test the weight of the mowed grass.
Now she opens her face to let you pass.

Without it, how could you find your way?
The stone basin you'd see, but not the light

making its shining climb up the windblown spray
of the fountain. You'd see its pivot and fall

but not the courage of shadows without bodies
or stones speaking in their uncrackable code.

You'd hear the dove call from the open gate,
but not the place where silence becomes the road.

Rooms

All winter the rooms of the forest stand empty.
Now light lives there, and comes and goes as she likes.
She has sold her furniture, which no one remembers.
The dogwoods arrange their ivory bowls on the air,
and clouds of leaves return to nest in the rafters.
The deer follow the stream from one room to the next.
The stream talks, and its talking scours the stones.
The skin of the river is cut into many small hills,
blond needles fall thick as hair under the pines,
where the comet that so many saw hang over the city
sailed each night in the still pond on the farm
yet left not a single track on its heavenly shore.
The mountains grow brighter and brighter—what can
    be in them?
Why do you knock, when you yourself are the door?

An Open Book

If the tree speaks true, the hills are holy
not for the tree's sake but for the road
unwinding this tale, if the road speaks true,

not for the story's sake but for the book
you hold in your hand, the pages turning
to hills, the road telling all,

the tree speaking
the glad words running to meet you.

A NOTE ABOUT THE AUTHOR

Nancy Willard grew up in Ann Arbor, Michigan, and was educated at the University of Michigan and Stanford University. She has written two novels, four books of stories and essays, and twelve books of poetry, including *Water Walker*, which was nominated for the National Book Critics Circle Award. A winner of the Devins Award, she has received NEA grants in both fiction and poetry. She teaches in the English department at Vassar College and lives in Poughkeepsie, New York.

A NOTE ON THE TYPE

The text of this book was set in Walbaum, a typeface designed by Justus Erich Walbaum in 1810. Walbaum was active as a typefounder in Goslar and Weimar from 1799 to 1836. Though the letter forms of this face are patterned closely on the "modern" cuts then being made by Giambattista Bodoni and the Didot family, they are of a far less rigid cut. Indeed, it is the slight but pleasing irregularities in the cut that give this typeface its human quality and account for its wide appeal. In its very appearance Walbaum jumps boundaries, having a look more French than German.

Composed by Creative Graphics, Inc.,
Allentown, Pennsylvania

Printed and bound by Rose Printing Company Inc.
Tallahassee, Florida

Designed by Soonyoung Kwon